True Love Stories

and other poems

Michael Creagan

True Love Stories
and other poems

ISBN 0-944933-12-2

DRAGONFLYER
press

Dragonflyer Press
592 North Euclid Avenue
Upland, California 91786
www.dragonflyerpress.com

Printed in Hong Kong

Dedication

For my children,
Sara and Rachel,
Michelle, John and Lindsey,
Sean and Michael.

For Heather and Andy and Gus,
and in loving memory of Phyllis.

For all my friends and fellow poets in Claremont.
Pete and Patty, Nancy and Frances,
Pat and Virginia.
For the gang at Yiannis,
the best little restaurant in Claremont,
Greg and Jimmy and Matt,
Stella and Bret and Rob.

For my dear friends and honorary family,
Bob and Ollie and Steve,
Naomi and Matt, and Jake, and in loving memory of Julien.

I dream of the perfect book.
The pages are all white.
There is not one word,
only the pure desire
nobody can read.

We wanted something else,
of course, but tell me how
we could have asked for this?

For Bob
with fond affection

Michael Geogan

Contents

Foreword

The arrangement of poems in the book is roughly chronological. I have been writing poems since my freshman year in college, where I was fortunate to have as a teacher, the poet, James Crenner, who had recently returned from Iowa University, where he had studied with Donald Justice. One day in class, he started writing some of Justice's poems on the blackboard, to illustrate some point about diction. That was the beginning of my vocation as a poet. I want to thank Jim Crenner for being so generous with his time while he was at St. Vincent. We spent many hours in his office talking about poetry, and going over my early poems, attempting to make them better. I received a fine education in the art of poetry. When he left to go back to Iowa, two years later, I was on my own. I went on reading and writing poetry, through busy years in medical school, the Army, and then the last 28 years in which I have worked as an emergency medicine specialist at San Antonio Community Hospital, in Upland, California.

Only two years ago, I met Bob Mezey, a poet I had read and admired since I started down the path of poetry. He was my virtual neighbor in Claremont, and welcomed me into the community of poets here. With his kind and generous help and encouragement, I have had the pleasure of seeing some of my poems in print during my lifetime, and, as I like to joke, have learned to relinquish my twisted dream of becoming the Emily Dickinson of Claremont.

Bob and Ollie have been unsparing in their help and encouragement, and this book would have been much the poorer without their help and wise criticism. I could never thank them enough.

I would like to thank Donald Justice and W. D. Snodgrass, poets who have been, for a long time, heroes of mine, and whose books I return to often, for instruction and delight.

I would also like to say how lucky I have been to have been able to work at San Antonio Community Hospital for so many years with such a good group of doctors, nurses, clerks, paramedics, techs, volunteers, and case managers, who work hard every day to take good care of the patients who come to the hospital for help. Thanks to George Kuykendall for introducing me to John Jopes

Thanks also to the folks at Dragonflyer Press, John and Carolyn, Chris and Digger, Erin and Tasha and Phillip.Thanks for wanting to publish my book.

Thanks to the editors of the books and magazines and papers in which many of these poems were first published. A special thanks to Jeffrey Hart, editor of the *National Review*, who has published several of my poems in the last two years.

Thanks to all the members of my family who have had to put up with my crazy work schedule and my obsession with poetry.

Enough. This book is now on its own.

After A Line By Donald Justice

the last line, but never used in a poem

Too long, you feel, the walls have kept you in.
And you know the walls. The walls are so thin.

There is a shoreless blackness, deeper than water,
that you have seen all day, that runs forever.

Beautiful leaves float on it in this weather.

You are frightened at the distance you have come
from somewhere, but where, you can't remember,
or why it was you left, if it was home.

You remember, long ago, running this fast,
the look of the fields when you were lost.

Going To Iowa

lines written when I was trying to decide whether to stay in medical school or go to the Writer's Workshop in Iowa to write poetry

To go all the way out there for *this*?
Writing poems is a strange business.
I might write of all the things I'd miss,
    in Iowa.

Could the land be flatter than what I'd write,
smoking and sweating, late every night,
to find some words that would be all right,
    in Iowa?

I'm naturally quiet anyway.
I would be nervous every day,
sitting around with nothing to say,
    in Iowa.

October's Child

You will be born soon.
I wait with such desire
and know it is not enough.
There are few words for fathers.
Sometimes I fear there is nothing
I can speak to you ever again,
having already dared
to ask you out of Heaven,
to come, darling, come
and burn in this fire.
O may your desire
be equally terrible.

Memories From Childhood: Drinking Fountain

One of the things I remember
is the fountain in the park,
the taste of the cold water
from the brass spigot, the splashing
into the stone basin,
the quiet sound of the drain,
and how wonderful it was
that the water had come miles,
running deep under the city
from the beautiful lakes,
inexhaustible reservoirs
shining far away.

Memories From Childhood: In The Attic

I wanted to know that everything is important
and nothing can ever be forgotten, or lost,
but things I loved would be lost in a place like this,
and that was only a small part of it.
Sometimes I would imagine I was a ghost
coming back to remember all these things:
old rifles, uniforms and bridal gowns,
diaries, love letters, fading photographs,
corsages crushed in books, broken violins.

Heart Attack

There is storm outside.
She thinks of her good father
in the hospital, and weeps.
The way she shudders with the lightning
you might think she was waiting
for the sound of a great heart breaking,
and she tells me that long ago,
safe on the porch from the rain,
she and her father would watch
the lightning and count the seconds
until the thunder came.

Going

Going away from you
into certain nights
brings back this nervousness
I can remember once,
getting out of the water
as night was coming on,
the cold wind moving
across the skin of the lake
where fish started up like goosepimples.

In The Hospital; Watching People Die

At first I expected them to go in anger,
or fear and trembling maybe, or raving with fever.
But there is no desperate calling on God or the devil
to fetch them one more time from out of trouble,
nor do they seem to be thinking of the Hell or Heaven
our elders warned us of when we were children.
Their hands are quiet and are not reaching at air
for something to hold onto, someone dear.
No, in fact, they seem not at all worried,
only disappointed, and very, very tired.

A Grave Poem For A Gift

You gave me an elephant,
an antique carved in ivory,
a sign, beautifully tiny,
of all we wished it meant.

I could wish it would grow beneath us
and lift us into the air.
On his wide back, we could soar
to the warmest Africas

and let him run or walk
through all love's steamy thickets
until snow fell in the tropics
or we broke his humping back.

But O such heartless giving
if on one ivory key
I should try and pluck someday
the whole tune of our loving.

My memory, out of tune,
unlike an elephant's,
would sorrowfully note what once
was real is dead and gone,

as everything I love
goes, as an elephant dies,
although we know it has
some hidden, priceless grave.

Learning To Talk

You will soon learn to talk.
I would like to hear you say
my name. But I am sorry,
for there is an old curse.

You will have thousands of words
and you will know what you know
and there will be whole years
when you say nothing at all.

Shark Attack On The Tennis Court

I am playing tennis with my son
who is eight years old and fascinated by sharks.
He wants the game to be a metaphor
for a shark attack. When he slams the ball to my left
and my weak backhand, he yells out something like:
I am the Great White Shark attacking my father
at his weakest point, my saw-like teeth
tearing his flesh to tiny, bloody pieces
which settle slowly to the ocean bottom.
I am really alarmed, but who would believe me
if I said I was hurt by a shark on the tennis court?
We go on playing tennis in the sun.
He slams the ball at me as hard as he can,
his racquet slashing toward me like a fin.

Wounds

One hand in bandages,
the child gathers his friends
so he can tell his story.

He put a needle in,
right into my thumb.
And then he took a knife
and cut away the infection
and the whole fingernail.
This pan was full of blood.
It hurt an awful lot,
but I didn't cry.

The child runs off to play,
the pain almost forgotten,
waving the gauze like a flag
that will set him apart forever.

It is painful to look back.
I am still a child.
There are innumerable wounds,
proud bandages.

Divorce

1. The safe and beautiful bridges into the future
   are blowing up before you can get across.
   After the battle, the body count is fiction.
   You are trying to get away, with the dead on your back,
   and you think you should report yourself as dead,
   if only you could remember who you are.
   If you have a life at all, it is a story
   you tell yourself, always making it up.
   Of course, it always was, but now you know it,
   and it comes apart, at night, in your bad dreams,
   in the separate houses, when you fall asleep.

2. I gave you a crystal ball.
   You saw a green field
   far away, where something
   was living. This frightened me.
   I think I have given my life
   over to dreams, but when
   I looked into the crystal,
   I had fallen so low
   I could summon none of them,
   I could see nothing at all.

3. Someday, in another life,
   finding a photograph,
   or a ring, or a lock of hair,
   I will remember you
   and be surprised into sadness,
   but I don't think it will feel
   like raking up a severed
   hand among the leaves,
   though I will be full of questions,
   as long ago, as a child,
   in one of the huge museums,
   when I would stand and look
   at the pale articulate bones,
   imagining dinosaurs.

4. I wish the distance between us
   would explain itself,
   but nothing will come of it.
   It feeds on itself, like someone
   who has been hurt very much,
   who opens his mouth to speak,
   and then remains silent.

5. It is hard to imagine a landscape
   in which this might ever happen,
   but I think it would be quiet,
   there would be enough light,
   and we would be still in love,
   neither hurt, nor angry, nor afraid,
   but proud of ourselves, our arms
   reaching out, our hands
   opening like flowers.

No One Should Write About Things Like This

The "Little King" was a character in the comics, long ago,
and I used his name as a term of endearment for my wife,
and sometimes with other things in mind

Bad dreams. The little king
wanted to cut off my head.
She gave me a silver ring.
I was as good as dead.

I ran so far away
I thought I could never come back.
In a dream, I heard her say,
I want to marry Jack.

The ring still hadn't vanished.
But I love you, I said.
I'm back. We're not finished.
I was as good as dead.

She was kind, tolerant,
but *I can't give up my life*
for something I don't want.
No dream. I've lost my wife.

I'm writing this down alone.
No love. Nobody's home.
Some monsters devour their own,
some use them for a poem.

On A Night Like Tonight

On a night like tonight, I am trying to enjoy
the life of contemplation, but then I get lost
on one of the dark boulevards of nostalgia,
and end up later in the neighborhood of fear and despair
where I watch a man without hands
attempting to button his coat against the wind.

The world is ugly and the people are sad
is a thought that comes to mind, and I repeat it,
with delusions of grandeur, with a broken heart.

My wife and children are gone. In the world of action
or the life of contemplation, nothing suffices.

On a night like tonight, I wish I had leukemia.

Wanting To Go All The Way Down

Out of the blue water
you fall through violet and black
to the blackest, and the light you carry
has nothing to reflect from,
only your own hands
if you bring them close to your face.
The bottom settles beneath you
and will not fall out.
You rise, slowly, to the air,
the bubbly surfaces.

"O This Is The Creature That Does Not Exist"

The world is here and staying all night.
But this is not enough. There is something else
that is always missing.
You think you knew what it was, long ago.
It was forgotten and it went away.
It went away and has forgotten you.
But now it comes so near,
as if just on the other side of a wall
in which a door might suddenly be made to open.

You look outside. Tonight there is a full moon
and the sky is so full of light
it seems almost holy, or unholy.
He or she or it is out there.
It must be so. You want it so much.

Hells

1.
He feels as if he were covered
with dust, as if the dust
were still slowly descending.

He thinks he would be afraid
to open the doors or windows,
or simply open his mouth.

There are no changes but the ones
that happen to us, he thinks,
and waits for something to happen.

2.
The windows are dirty. He cleans them
and is sorry. All he can see
outside are dirty windows.

He imagines what is beyond them
and beyond then and beyond them,
up to the last window.

He wonders why it is there,
or if it *is* there,
and begins to throw rocks.

3.
Under bandages, he conceals
a terrible wound, which he
uncovers each night, in secret.

It happened long ago.
He no longer remembers why.
His hand goes into it.

When he is satisfied,
new bandages are provided.
The wound must never heal.

A Shell

A shell, washed up by water into sun,
recalls the water, whispering its sound.

But you, my skull, my bone, how will you keep
the memory of this dream when I am gone?

Variations

1.
He would spend a long time
preparing the instruments
for the one symphony only

when the music that there is
would desire to hear itself
and start the bows moving

across the perfect strings,
give breath to the woodwinds and horns,
send batons down to the drums,

except that the music is deaf
and has no desire,
the instruments would never suffice.

Already he detects
squeaks in the highest ranges,
a hollowness in the percussion,

an incorrectable,
disturbing tendency
towards a pervasive flatness.

And the only music he gets
is that of his own desire
(mutilated so?)

for that other music
which has no desire
and can never be written.

2.
I dream of the perfect book.
The pages are all white.
There is not one word,
only the pure desire
nobody can read.

3.
Desire wanders over
the lost snows of itself,
dazzled and frozen,
dreaming of sleep.

Droppings, these lines,
black marks over the snow,
making the trail of a beast
who would want to follow?

On The Literature Of Suicide Notes

They are often found
by the police who state
that the contents will not be disclosed.

It is tempting to assume
that the notes are dangerous,
or even magical,

that they cannot be destroyed,
that the policemen who read them
succumb to a fatal madness,

and that their gifted authors
had been working for years
to finish the impossible,

perfect explanation
that would leave them nothing to live for,
that would, in fact, kill them,

since within their own words
they would finally see God.
No one can see him twice.

Fantasy Of The Mad Poet

It is very quiet,
the setting in which I imagine
I write my last poem,
having burned all the others.

I am beginning to die,
composing the perfect note
for a suicide. The poem
will take me effortlessly.

I will not be found,
only my poem. No one
will read it more than once.

In The Museum Of The Mad Poet

This is the room he slept in
and the bed where he made love
with his wife, on the dates engraved
on the small gold plate attached
to the headboard.

These are the glasses he wore
whenever he went out.
The lenses are made of lead.

This is his diary, locked,
with its two entries, written
twenty years apart;

and these, his collected letters
to friends. They were never mailed.
All the pages are blank.

This is the fireplace
in which he revised his poems.

And the poem he wrote the night
he died is in that vault
on the other side of all
the ropes and guards provided
by the state.

The Mad Poet Reconsiders His Position

The white page was once
the holy absolute.
Writing was blasphemous.
Now I think of the page
as simply a blank page
a poem can be written on.
Or the page is white noise
that can be tuned into music,
or the fresh sheets of a bed
where something lovely can happen.
This is because I have fallen
in love. I recommend it
for anyone who writes.
It is fun to rescue poems
from oblivion, and name them,
and they do the same for you,
and they wake you up each morning
so you have to make it happen
and you want to make it happen
again and again and again.

The Master Sketches The World One Afternoon

Now he puts his brush
away. The black ink
dries on the white paper.

He has left nothing out
this time, not one spider
or one cloud. A great

wind starts up. The ink
spills across the paper.
Then the sky darkens.

He is taken into the night.

Magical Poem

Night is the sky over this poem.
It is too black for stars.
And do not look for any illumination.
                              –Donald Justice

A door opens and a man enters the room.
He sits down at his desk and begins to write,
and I do the same, in a room across the street.
Our windows face each other. We wave hello.

I am writing a poem about the sky
that was so strange and beautiful tonight
(such blue shot through with pink, as the sun went down),
it cast its magic over everyone.

Let that sky be the sky over this poem.
I've had it with starless nights, portentous moons,
and poems that are always final and sad.
Let that sky be the sky over this poem!

Let it make something truly amazing happen!
The poem is charmed. It is becoming happy.
I am happy and I don't know why.
I look up at my friend across from me

and suddenly we both know what has happened.
We run out into the street and exchange our poems.
We have written the same poem! This is the poem!
We embrace and join hands and begin dancing.

The neighbors come out of their houses and applaud.

Publishing

No longer hooked on their lines,
still I print my poems,
showing my helpless love
for the cages I've broken out of,
the coops I've built and flown.

Poem Smoking A Cigarette In A Dark Corner Of The Page

I am not about to answer your question
in this poem. There is a certain amount
of mystery in any good relationship
which is not to be confused with misunderstanding.

Or would you like to see the abominable snowman
on the Johnny Carson show, talking about
his cameo appearance in the Ice Capades?

The Silence Of Books

The silence of books is like
the sound of the tree falling
deep in the empty forest.

Will the book ever tell its story?
Will anything ever happen?
Now you open the book

and begin to read. Now
you can hear the tree falling
deep in the empty forest,

now the words on the page
flare up, like coals when the wind comes.

Writing Poetry, After Reading B. F. Skinner

No one knows what's in the black box.
The black box is the mind, the secret jewel.
The world buzzes by, polishing it
with positive and negative reinforcers.
I had to write this poem. I deserve no credit.
Mental event are not irrelevant,
but private, like o rgasms. You cannot see them
and it is useless to talk about them at all
with inaccurate, introspective vocabularies.
All you can see is my hand holding the pen,
my hand moving the pen across the page.
The poem becomes part of the environment.
You can guess what you want, but it doesn't matter
and I can't tell you any more than this:
I write these poems because it feels so good.

Why There Is A Monument Named After Him

We know he cut down cherries as a boy,
although the books all say he'd never lie.

He fathered the country, made that his career.
Word has it he slept almost everywhere.

How hard it must have been to get that done.
Erect a phallus, then, for Washington.

Dry Lament

And though I know I'll never find the reason
that, without reason, I have from Heaven
this curse I struggle under, being human,
I know, for what it's worth, the curse is common.

Platonic Monologue

Tell your one, should she presume to complain
about your many, that they are false. Explain
that knowing them brings knowledge, though unsure,
which in the end will lead you back to her.

Alba

After the line: Ah God, ah God, the dawn, it comes how soon.
                                                    –French, 12th century

Not long ago,
When last the sun
Put down his head,
Leaving us to bed
To get undone,
Let warm blood flow
And headway make, as lovers know,
I thought of dawn,
How it would come
Before I'd come and gone
Enough, and then some,
How the cock, bright red,
Would scream, and said:
Ah God, ah God, the dawn, it comes how soon.

Helplessly,
We rode all night.
Were you a horse,
Begging your pardon, of course,
And I a knight,
I swear that we,
From France, could have made Italy.
I thought of dawn,
Wished it would come
Before my flesh was gone
Or torn, or numb.
Frantic, half-dead,
Still dying, I said:
Ah God, ah God, the dawn, it comes how soon?

At last it came.
At last I rose
And got away.
I thought of you all day,
Pulling on clothes,
Calling my name.
Lady, you'll never be the same.
Neither will I, glad to tell.
I think that bye and bye,
Tonight as well,

I will return,
Again to learn,
Ah God, ah God, the dawn, it comes how soon.

Anatomy Lesson

The anatomy professor
picks up a piece of chalk
and carefully draws on the blackboard
the larynx of a pig.

The larynx of a pig
has the same anatomy
as the larynx of a man.
Then why does the pig not speak?

The pig has nothing to say.

The Problem Of Brain Research

The light he calls his own
may be going out,

but in its own darkness
it keeps on turning on flashing

like an animal chasing its tail,
only more beautiful,

the light wanting to shine
only upon itself.

Hypochondria

Good news. Your electrocardiogram is normal.
The chest X-ray is normal. The blood tests are normal.
That pain in your chest is nothing serious.
But the patient looks at you as though you had slapped him.
Are you trying to say there is nothing wrong with me?

You try again: I am sorry to have to tell you
that your X-ray revealed an incurable lung cancer.
You will suffer a protracted and horribly painful death.
To the family, you say: There is nothing we can do.
If he were a dog, it would be kind to shoot him.

His eyes shine, an unhealthy radiance.
The curtain rises on the final act
and he is at center stage, playing the part
that he has been rehearsing all his life.
Now he is happy. Now he has something to live for.

Side Effects

More doctors used to smoke Camels
than any other cigarette.
Kinder to the T zone, indeed.

Think of the children of mothers
who used Thalidomide,

or the workers in plastic factories,
dying of cancer of the liver.

Now spray cans are destroying the ozone layer
and you can start to worry about your own skin.

Fewer men would lose their hair
if all men were castrated before puberty.

Perhaps the occasional use of aspirin
impairs the mind's ability to recall
certain shades of lavender.

Perhaps drinking milk
makes people more philosophic about death.

Do not touch me, friend.
When I am old,
I might remember you
and weep.

Would you really be surprised
if an atmospheric pollutant
made flowers bloom from your fingertips?

What are the side effects of these poems?

Memory

O recreate that hour
Divine Mnemosyne,
When all things to the eye
Their early splendors wore.
                    −Donald Justice

This prayer runs through my mind while I am attending
a medical convention in San Diego.
From the balcony outside my hotel room, I look across
at hundreds of balconies exactly the same as my own,
at hundreds of gleaming cars in the parking lot,
at a kidney-shaped pool, on the grounds of the grand hotel,
surrounded by grass, by the occasional palm tree.

The hotel reminds me that there are too many people.
The cars remind me of the energy problem
and the problems of mass transit and air pollution.
The swimming pool makes me think of water pollution,
water shortages and kidney diseases.
Palm trees always remind me of French ticklers.

That early splendor depended on ignorance.
When you try to remember, there is too much to forget.

The International Ballroom Dancing Competition

I am sitting in a restaurant with a friend.
I tell him how happy I am to be a physician,
how it satisfies all my needs, how I'm never bored.
Then a large group of middle-aged people sit down
at the next table. The sound excited, talking
about the International Ballroom Dancing
Competition. A couple from Venezuela
were utterly fantastic in the rumba.
They have been out dancing tonight, embellishing
their skills in the rumba, the samba, the mambo, the tango,
the foxtrot, the cha cha, the waltz and God knows what.
I try to imagine a ballroom, and all I can think of
is a dim room where a multifaceted ball
of tiny mirrors hangs from the center of the ceiling,
reflecting some colored lights, which gleam also
in the polished surface of a muted trumpet
and a saxophone. I think of diagrams
of black footprints, from Arthur Murray ads.
When I try to think of a rumba, my mind is blank.
I am suddenly depressed, telling my friend
that medicine takes up too much of my goddamn time.
There are so many kinds of human experience
I will never have time for, and in relation to which
I will always remain a complete and utter failure.

Fragment

God is speaking to his psychiatrist:
I want to forget about the universe.
Each morning I create it all again
after blowing it to bits the night before.
Each day I watch what happens, hoping this time
things will turn out differently. But no,
history always ends up repeating itself,
down to the last detail. I have watched this happen
at least a million times. I'm sick of it.
You should see what happens on earth. Late each morning,
the human race appears. I hold my breath.
A short time later, they are dropping bombs on each other.
This is bad enough, but other things
have started to bother me in my old age.
Out of the magical cloud, heavy with promise,
out of creation's egg, always the same
weird characters appear, like recurrent nightmares.
There is an old fakir in India
who charms cobras out of a wicker basket
with a flute. He and the cobra rise up,
eye to eye, their heads swaying together,
and then the fakir suddenly drops his flute
and bites the cobra's head off and spits it out.
Each day I watch this Russian work for years
to write his name on a single human hair.
Each day I listen to a man in France
sing through his anus. And all the insane poets.
Each day I watch my marvellous creation
degenerate into a sideshow. It depresses me.
What do I want to happen? I don't know.
But each day, like clockwork, the wrong things happen.
Always, by afternoon, Beethoven is deaf.
Nixon is always elected president.
It's not funny, I know, but can't stop laughing.
I appeared to that man in Kansas, the same one,
pretending to be a monster from outer space,
and he was friendly, as usual, and gave me coffee,
but I can't talk to him. And later, as usual,
he went home and shot his wife and kids and the dog.
I was telling my wife last night, their terrible history

is a nightmare from which I'm afraid I will never awaken.
Now I even beginning to sound like them.
O gods of forgetfulness attend to me
and bless me into a deep and dreamless sleep.

Prose Poem

I meet an old friend on the street and we go into a restaurant. Both of us order coffee. When the waitress brings the coffee, my friend says: I've changed my mind. I would rather have some tea. The waitress brings the tea and then my friend tells me didn't really want either coffee or tea. She was only doing her homework for her weekly class in how to be assertive. She tells me: I am learning how to be selfish in the good sense. I respect myself. I go to singles bars and start up conversations with strange men and I don't feel compelled to go home with them. In fact, it is fun to say "No," and watch the expression on their faces. We have all kind of neat exercises to do for homework. I go into restaurants all the time and ask for a glass of water and order nothing else. She laughs. I also go into a lot of places and ask to use the bathroom. I shop for clothes for hours and never feel any pressure to buy anything. And sometimes I buy clothes with the deliberate intention of bringing them back later. All of this may sound silly, but I really think it has helped me to feel much better about myself. I was finally able to ask my boss for a raise, and I got it. And I'm starting to feel more comfortable about sharing some of my sexual fantasies. With the right people, of course. We finish our coffee and tea. I say I have to go. She pays the check and complains to the man at the cash register that her tea was cold. Outside the restaurant, she asks if she can take me out to dinner tonight, and I say "No," and she smiles at me and I smile back. And perhaps she thinks we are smiling at the little irony present in this exchange, but I think I am smiling because I have been thinking, over and over, throughout this whole conversation: *Someday the sun will burn out.*

The Man With The Biggest Telephone Bill
In The World

He lived alone, but there
was a phone in his room. One night
he read somewhere that *the world*

is an incessant web of signals.
He thought this was probably true
and picked up his phone. He imagined

telephone wires extending
into the night, like a vast
anatomy of nerves.

Each number he dialed would connect him
to someone else. He decided
to call up everybody.

At the end of the first month,
his telephone bill was as thick
as the New York City phone book.

They disconnected his phone,
after calling an ambulance.
Safe in the hospital now,

he sits alone on the sun porch
dialing the air all day
with his right index finger.

An amazing repertoire
of clicks, rings and dial tones
issues from his throat.

No matter what the other
patients say to him,
he only answers either:

You have the wrong number,
Buddy, or: *If you ever*
try to talk to me
again, I'll call the police.

The Interpretation Of Dreams

I had a dream last night in which I consulted a neurologist
because of certain problems with perception and thinking.
After an examination, he said I needed surgery
on a small part of my brain in the back of my head.
There had been a small amount of internal bleeding.
It was probably still going on. I was amazed.
When I asked what had caused it, he said he wasn't certain,
but he suspected that someone had come into my bedroom,
when I was asleep, and hit me on the head
with a lead pipe. He scheduled me for surgery.

Today I mentioned the dream to a Jungian analyst
who looked embarrassed and muttered something about
the strangeness of dreams in general. I asked my wife
for her interpretation. She only smiled,
and said I should try to figure it out for myself.

Today I met a girl with a scar on her leg.
I asked her about the scar. When she was ten years old,
she was riding her bike on the sidewalk in front of her house
when a plane fell out of the sky and crashed in the street.
A wing brushed her leg it went past.
I asked her if she had any bad dreams
because of this, and she said that she had.

Then I read about a man who had fallen from a ladder
and struck his head. He had been perfectly normal,
but after he injured his head, he became clairvoyant.
He thought there was a mechanism for this talent
in everybody's brain, and that his accidental fall
had turned this mechanism on, something like
slamming a TV to make a fine adjustment in the reception.

For a long time, I have thought of myself as somehow different.
Once, a complete stranger came up to me
in a hospital cafeteria and invited me
into a secret circle of magicians and mystics.
He said he could recognize a certain look in my eyes.
I politely declined, but I never forgot what he said.

I remember, a long time ago, waking up
with a really terrible headache. I never have headaches.

I think that someone came into my room one night,
when I was asleep, and hit me on the head with a lead pipe.

Variations On A Theme

1. What is beautiful?
    This is hard enough,
    but Aesthetics will never explain
    the sweet lure of the secrets
    under Beauty's dress.

2. I remember a day in the attic
    when I was ten years old.
    Turning the pages, I found
    the black and white illustrations
    in the gynecology book.

    Perhaps this explains why today,
    when I open any book,
    I tremble with excitement,
    looking for revelations,
    rare epiphanies.

3. The hormones of adolescence
    are mind-altering drugs
    I suddenly found myself
    in a parked car, one night,
    crazy with desire
    simply to touch something

    which might as well have been
    as far away as the moon,
    the moon that stared through the windshield
    like a policeman's flashlight.

4. The clitoris is the only
    organ in the body
    of either sex whose only
    function is pure pleasure.

    The Book Of Genesis
    omits the story of God
    dreaming the clitoris.

I am not religious,
but whenever God is described
as a stern and angry father,
I like to think of this.

5. It is the door to this world.
    It causes terrible dreams.

    It is Pandora's box
    and Eve's seductive apple,
    the vagina dentata, the wound
    that bleeds with the moon's rhythms,
    that wound that never heals.

    The darkness we escaped from
    we always want to back to.

    You are a poem on the tip of my tongue,
    I have tried. There is no way to say this.

Dream On A Rainy Day

It is a rainy day,
a good day for sleeping,
I tell myself. The rain
drums me back to sleep
I have a didactic dream:
I walk out the front door
of my house into the rain,
forgetting my hat and coat
and wearing the unmistakable
look of a fanatic.
I splash along the streets
of old, dark houses,
ignoring my friends who offer
umbrellas and hot coffee.
When I get to the edge of town,
I walk up the face of a mountain,
take off my wet clothes
and enjoy a few minutes
of ceremonial dancing.
The sharp rain whips me
into a fine frenzy,
before a bolt of lightning
introduces me to the crowd.

I am about to begin
a long, general confession
in spontaneous blank verse,
in which I will say out loud
my most secret wish,
the one I am not aware of.
I am saved from all of this
by my wife, who has been patiently
pouring cold water
over my face, saying:
All you do is sleep.
I shudder to think of it.
It is still raining.

So Much Light

The single rose in the vase
is losing its petals fast.
I pick one of them up.
It is not delicate,
but elastic and tough, like skin,
like a severed eyelid.
I knew someone once
who had cut off both of his eyelids
because of love or fear
or a sense of obligation.
There was suddenly so much light,
he remembered. And there were tears,
but not nearly enough.
His corneas became steamy
with scars, and then opaque.
At noon on the brightest day,
he could only see shadows.
You could see him tapping his way
along the street, terrible
dark clouds in his eyes.
Sometimes he would walk
across the lawns and gardens
and pause to move his fingers,
gently, over the faces
of children, the petals of flowers.

World War II

Grandfather is telling him
war stories again.
He tells him about the night
on the aircraft carrier,
somewhere in the Pacific,
when enemy planes came over.
The lights were all blacked out
on the carrier,
and the radio transmitter
was turned off.
The receiver was still on
and messages could come in.
One plane was flying back
to the carrier.
It called in on the radio
asking for lights on the runway
and permission to land.
Grandfather was the radio operator,
the men in the lost plane were his friends,
but all he could do was listen.
The plane ran out of fuel
and went down in the water.
"But tell me what they said."
"I can't remember anymore."

The child goes off to bed,
but now he knows what to do
with the broken radio
up in the attic. Tomorrow,
he will turn it on,
and the dusty tubes will glow
with an orange light, and then
he can listen to the silence
after the plane had gone down.

I Am So Happy I Could Die

I would usually tell you
that things are already bad
and steadily getting worse.
But I am happy now
and nothing bothers me.
This happiness has descended
on me like grace. I have done
nothing to deserve it,
and it depends on nothing
that can be taken away.
Tonight I imagine the sky
as the interior of a bell
where the moon swings back and forth
with the rhythm of a heart,
or a slow loving rhythm.
Each time the bell is struck,
the world is created again,
but there is no sound at all,
only this thrill in the bones,
the thrill of being alive
and in love with it. And I think
if the world should end tonight,
the stars fall from the sky,
it would be all right, it would be
like snow in July, another
unexpected blessing.

Soliloquy Of The Birthday Party Magician

I know how the great Houdini
made the elephant vanish
on the stage of the Hippodrome.

I'm happy making coins
and oranges disappear
in front of the amazed

faces of children. For them
I endure the uncouth rabbits
who often shit in my hat,

and for them I'm sometimes ashamed
of the rubber bands in my sleeves,
the flesh-toned shells on my fingers.

Tired of these illusions,
anyone might wish
for another kind of magic.

I understand why Crowley
entered the magic circle
for his invocations,

and why Houdini looked years
for someone who could tell him
how to escape from death.

I am also afraid of death.
We are like the doves,
trembling, in his pockets.

But Crowley went raving mad,
talking to himself
in the middle of the desert;

and Houdini was disappointed;
always the hands of the spirit
were fashioned out of wax.

It is difficult not to wish
for another kind of magic.
Nonetheless, I'm in love

with the magic that there is.
I have been close to despair
but I am always amazed.

Rain falls from the sky
and a flower blooms in the dirt.
Women bring forth children

and the sun pulls the world each morning
out of night's black hat,
so I am beside myself

and practice my tricks again,
all my splendid illusions,
my grand metaphors.

I have practiced for so long,
standing in front of my mirrors,
I can almost fool myself.

You should see what I can do
with my silk handkerchiefs,
my mysterious Chinese sticks,

my rings, my magic wands.
I would never tell you
this is not real magic.

The Night Of The UFO Sighting

Tonight a farmer reported
that a flying saucer had landed
in the woods next to his barn.
Hundreds of people came
and helped the local police
explore the woods, hoping
to discover the flying saucer
or a patch of scorched grass,
or the imprint of a landing pod
in the mud. From the top of a hill,
overlooking the woods,
I could see their flashlights and lanterns
moving back and forth
below me in the darkness.
They found nothing, of course.

I am from outer space.
I am a million years old.
There are no flying saucers,
but I have lived here for years
and I can understand
why they have been dreamed up
by these people, whose small lives
are shadowed by pathos and dread.
I will live forever
and I have my own dreams.
Tonight when I went to bed,
I floated out of my body
over Pennsylvania.

I saw the design of cities,
I watched the brain of an ant.
I saw all the bones in the earth
and the bones above the earth,
buried in flesh. I saw
what happens when a man dies.
I saw a man and woman
making love, and heard
what they promised each other tonight,
and saw how the promises would be

broken. I could hear,
deep in the bodies of women,
the quiet sound of conception.
I saw the sleeping faces
of children. The air was thick
with dreams. I understood
the past and future explained
in this one night. I saw things
I cannot explain in this language.
I saw a flock of birds
with moonlight on their wings.
I saw the moon reflected
in a thousand lakes.

It was all so beautiful,
and it was almost enough,
but when I went out to the woods
tonight, I wanted to see
a flying saucer, or I wanted
something unimaginable
to happen, and it never does.

The Brilliant Room

You are escorted into
the brilliant room to wait
for the person with the answers.

You are going to find out why
you had an unhappy childhood,
why your marriage failed.

Finally you will hear
the answers to all the old
enigmas, including your favorite:

*Why is there something and not
nothing?* Here comes the person
with all the answers. What happens

next is pure chaos.
Suddenly you are exhorted
in millions of languages

no one has ever heard of,
though you think you recognize
some phrases of Latin and Greek.

In spite of yourself, you laugh,
you weep, you begin to dance
and sing. But after a while,

you realize there is unlimited
energy here and, after
all, you have your limits.

This preposterous,
you say to yourself, as you leave
the brilliant room. You hear,

Keep up the good work.

Consultation

The girl blows her nose and tells me:
Doctor, my nose is running and my throat hurts
and I've been coughing so much
I couldn't get to sleep all night.
What do think I have?

Christ, this is serious,
I think to myself, thinking of something else,
but she is waiting for my opinion so I tell her:
You have beautiful blue eyes.

Night

The poppies fold their petals when night comes.
I have seen it happen. I am jealous.
I have been trying to close up all night long.

I feel like a service station, somewhere in Kansas,
open all night, where some deluded bastard
thinks he is going to improve himself
by reading the encyclopedia through.

Three blocks away, you are sleeping with someone else.
This peace is not experienced as peaceful.

It is dark. It is beginning to rain.

Looking For Metaphors In The Mountains

These crazy birds zooming around our heads,
almost as quick as thoughts, could be our thoughts,
and so could the monstrous shadows of the clouds,
coming, like patches of night, across the mountains.
And the bushes of flowers by the fire road
could be your dreams, dreams I want for you
when you remember this, when you are gone,
dreams that bloom all night like wildflowers.
Even here in the desert, here on this mountain,
they conjure blossoms out of earth and water,
blossoms of pink and white and blue and gold.
And no one comes to gather flowers here,
but still they labor to be beautiful,
or more amazing, labor not at all
but simply are like this, like a burning bush
or quiet fireworks, Roman candles
always exploding, never coming down.

Long Distance

There is a shell,
an imaginary shell,
convoluted, pale,
all in my mind,
and it *is* my mind.
When I listen,
there is a sound like the sound that a shell makes
when you hold it close to your ear.
It is not the sound
of the Pacific,
or the sound of my own blood,
but a voice,
that must be your voice,
whispering,
deep
in the pink interior.

This is how you teach me this poem.
This is why I stay up all night,
writing it down for you

Why I Dropped Everything And Drove To Maine

Wyoming was beautiful.
Nebraska was a bitch.
The country went by like this,
and there I was in Maine,
with a sheepish smile on my face.
I had driven three thousand miles
to give this woman a kiss,
like the last foolish romantic,
and proud of it, of course.

The Foolish Romantic Has A Vision

Huge crates of china
and linen and crystal
are sinking into the lake.

The bride surfaces
on the back of a white horse,
who gallops out of the water
and heads for the distant hills,
after dropping a note at my feet.

It is a form letter.
To Whom It May Concern:
You were born to love this woman.
I am taking her far away.
I am not coming back.

I throw myself into the water
and begin to calm down.
I have always been sad.
Now I know why.
This begins to make my happy.
I forget how to drown.

Post Coitus, Etc.

No sadness should follow this,
but no matter where I look
I can see that you are missing,
my cock seems ridiculous
taken out of context,
and I feel lost in this bed
with only your name in my mouth,
my hands incredibly empty.

Goodbye, Goodbye

I haven't been this sad
since someone died. Going
away from you is about
as easy as waltzing out
of my own body and never
coming back. We have always
been happy. No one wants
to be sad. I could get
so desperate for some happy
solution, I might drink
the bottle of Joy over
by the sink, and blow
huge, delicate bubbles
out of my mouth for weeks
so I could die laughing.
If you act happy, then
you are happy, no matter
how you feel, I tell
myself, trying to salvage
my life as a relatively
slow-paced comedy,
though each minute it threatens
to degenerate into a painfully
lugubrious soap opera.
Meanwhile, my art is becoming
a convalescent home
for the perennially broken-hearted.
Like right now, I am locked
in my cabin trying to say
goodbye, but writing this poem
as if my life depended
on it, and it does.

Snowy Night One Year From Now

It is a year from now.
Pamela is standing
in a pale circle of light,
on a snowy street,
a street I have never seen,
in Amherst, Massachusetts.
She is waiting for someone.
It seems as if the snow
has been coming down for years
and will keep on falling,
and the person she is expecting
will never arrive. The night
is like a ball of glass
in which you can watch the snow
falling softly forever
into the perfect stillness
of a scene such as this,
where nothing can ever change.
You hold it in your hand.
You are excluded forever.

I will never arrive
to touch Pamela,
in the pale circle of light,
on a street I have never seen.
But it is not easy
to look away. The snow
catches fire, like stars,
in the dark sky of her hair.

Love Letter

After I learned the language,
I wanted to say something else,
but couldn't think of it.

After the masked ball,
I wanted to take off my face,
but I was stuck with it.

Believe me.
I am not the mad poet.
I am not the foolish romantic.

I am Michael.
I want to tell you I love you
in a language nobody knows.

Moonlight

Perhaps only the moonlight
remembers tonight

the secret path
into the dark woods,

the gold rings that are lost,
that shine under the surface
of forgotten lakes,

the silent attics,
the broken violins,

the empty cages
in the zoos of your childhood,

the overgrown outfields
of deserted stadiums,

the slow orbiting
of abandoned spaceships.

Confessions

I was a pole vaulter.
I am afraid of heights.

I played the clarinet,
but could never read music.

On my wedding night,
I dreamed of someone else.

I think of myself as a writer.
I love the white page.

Someday I will be dead.
I want to live forever.

Taking A Walk On Sunday

Today we walked through the quiet streets of Claremont
and the sunlit, park-like grounds of the colleges
with their wide lawns and monumental trees.
Over our heads was a sky of the clearest blue,
like the clear blue sky of the mind over the page,
and as we walked, with the sunlight warm on our skin,
it was easy, for once, to feel important and good,
as if we were being read, and understood.

When We Fell In Love

When we fell in love, we thought we had found a way
to understand history, and our own biographies.
Afterwards, we were perplexed, but no more than usual.

The lovers come together and kiss
for the first time, then for the last time.
We were the lovers, not believing it.
Where in these events would you locate the most sadness?

I think of the way a friend described his marriage:
A thousand and one nights of mercy fucks.

Sure, life can be dull,
but some some mornings you wake up happy
for no reason at all,
or a tree you thought was dead
blossoms overnight,
suddenly beautiful.
And still the future stretches out
to the cloudbank of oblivion on the horizon
like a minefield of pleasant surprises,
an occasional triumph of hope
over experience.
Which is why we want to live forever.

And still somewhere inside you
is the child running in circles,
feeling for the first time what it's like
to think about *forever*
and *never again.*

We wanted something else,
of course, but tell me how
we could have asked for this?

Anosmia

If you're legally blind, you can carry a white cane.
If you lose your sense of smell, who gives a damn?
I lost my sense of smell twelve years ago
after three operations on my nose
to remove nasal polyps. Now I can breathe,
but my mucous membranes are scarred and respond to nothing.
Millions of molecules bounce off their hard walls,
but no lights come on in my olfactory lobes.

I live now in Claremont, California.
Flowers are everywhere, and citrus trees,
but I walk down the beautiful, blooming streets
amusing myself by recalling the fond memory
of my last aroma, in 1966:
a trash can, under a fire escape, in Pittsburgh.

After Reading *The Closing Of The American Mind*
On A Visit To Hawaii

Tonight the tourists chatter at the luau
drowning out the muted cries of the peacocks.
A man from Ohio, who says he "in computers,"
is telling dirty jokes to a couple from Kansas.

I walk around, listening to conversations,
and get the impression that most of the people here
hate their husbands, their wives, their jobs, even their children.
I have no idea what they love.

How wonderful it is to contemplate the banality of evil
in a setting of such natural beauty, and to sit on the beach,
as I did this afternoon, reading an angry book
that attacks the university system in America

for failing to provide a truly classical education.
Even in a democracy, hell is other people,
not the long perspectives on the failure of culture,
or the incorrigibility of human nature,

but these perspectives alter your perceptions, and suddenly
a bunch of people enjoying their vacation
becomes an object lesson in the decline of civilization.
Back at the luau, the idiot from Ohio

is telling another joke, and the wife from Kansas
spills her colorful drink on her husband's shirt.
The tourists are getting louder. Looking for peace and quiet,
I walk down the winding path to the beach

and let the warm trade winds, blowing off the Pacific,
soothe my fevered brain, and my bad sunburn.
I think of Demosthenes standing on a beach
with pebbles in his mouth, making himself speak

loudly and clearly over the sound of the waves.
What did he have to say that was so important?
Someone walking by lights a cigar
and a cloud of smoke floats up

into the warm, tropical sky
like the soul leaving the body.
The stars shine like the eyes of the ancients.
Everybody decides to go for a swim.

Later tonight, when everyone is sleep,
there is an earthquake in Los Angeles
and small waves start out on their long journey.
Socrates drinks his hemlock, and asks for more.

True Love Stories

1. My mother and father are walking through Edgewood Park
   the night before their wedding, a night in June,
   in New Haven, in 1943.
   Walking behind them is my Aunt Loretta,
   my father's maiden aunt from Illinois,
   a silent, uninvited chaperone.
   She explained to my angry mother after the wedding
   she had wanted my parents to have no chance that night
   to do anything they might regret later,
   regret perhaps for all their married lives.
   My mother has never forgiven her for this.
   My father thinks that it was none of her business
   but "her heart was probably in the right place."

2. Forty years later, I drive by Edgewood Park
   on an autumn visit to Connecticut.
   An October evening, and the lights of New Haven are on,
   but the park looms in the middle of the city
   like a black forest. When I was a child,
   it seemed the sun was always shining down
   on the playground, the woods and meadows, the little duck pond;
   so it feels strange to see the park like this,
   dark and forbidding, abandoned for the night.
   The park was my enchanted forest once.
   And for my parents, it must have been enchanted
   when they walked through the park the night before their wedding.

   My mother and father are walking through Edgewood Park
   the night before their wedding, a night in June,
   in New Haven, in 1943.

   The bright glare of sunlight has softened to dusk
   and the air is rich with the scent of earth and flowers
   as they walk together down the wide dirt path.
   They stop in the shadows of a giant elm
   to kiss each other, then continue down the path,
   holding hands, talking, laughing a little,
   once in a while looking up at the sky
   where the moon and stars are becoming visible,
   once in a while looking over their shoulders

at Aunt Loretta. Perhaps they both are dreaming
of their wedding night, perhaps they are dreaming
of the children they will love together,
perhaps they are both dreaming about me.
As they walk along the path, now silvered with moonlight
and vanishing up ahead in the dark shadows,
do they think they will always be in love like this?
Of course they do, but that is another story.

This is how I like to imagine them
at the beginning of their love story
before the acid of time could start its work.
But they are still together, and still in love.
And I have been driving in circles around New Haven
dreaming about the world before I was born
and wondering how the powers of luck and love
can conjure someone out of oblivion
to *the million-petalled flower of being here.*
But here I am, feeling lucky and loved,
in a world as full of mystery as ever.
I doubt that anyone walks through the park tonight.
It's a cold night, and rain is starting to fall,
and I turn on the windshield wipers, and drive on.

3. When I was ten, I wanted to give my father
   a valentine that I had made at school;
   a big red heart pasted on white paper
   on which I had written the words, DAD, I LOVE YOU.
   I was too shy to give him the valentine,
   so I folded it carefully into a paper airplane
   and launched it toward him as he sat in his favorite chair
   reading a story to my sister Ellen.
   I watched as the valentine struck him in the forehead
   and tumbled into his lap. He picked it up,
   not looking at it, and crumpled it into a ball,
   then threw it at me, hitting me in the chest,
   with a look on his face so angry and unforgiving
   that I frightened myself by feeling I didn't love him.
   I picked up the valentine and ran to my room,
   and lay on my bed, sobbing. My father came in,
   and discovered what had happened, and held me tight,
   and I held onto him, but couldn't stop crying.

4. Eighty years old, my great-uncle Pierre
   was slowly dying of leukemia
   in a hospital, in Springfield, Massachusetts.
   Aunt Evelyn was with him day and night
   because she had been a nurse, because she loved him.
   One day she was trying to feed him some rice pudding
   but she was almost blind, and time after time,
   she would jab my uncle with spoonfuls of rice pudding
   on his forehead, on his nose, or in his eyes.
   Soon his face was covered with rice pudding.
   "I can't take this anymore," he said,
   and then he turned his face to the wall, and died.

5. My wife had been afraid of wolves since childhood
   when she had recurring dreams of the same wolf
   who would wait outside her window, night after night,
   howling and drooling. She would wake up screaming
   and her mother and father would tell her the wolf was gone
   but even when she was awake, she knew he was there.
   When we went to the Pittsburgh Zoo, I could feel her tremble
   as we walked past the wolves pacing in their cages.
   Intense fear like this can be contagious.
   I saw a wolf who was standing still in his cage
   and thought that he was staring at my wife.

   In the fourth year of our marriage, for a birthday present,
   someone had sent my name to one of those places
   that will investigate your family tree
   and prepare an official-looking document
   with the crest and shield of your distant ancestors.
   I was home with my wife when these treasures arrived in the mail,
   and we opened the large envelope together.
   On my family's shield, the heraldic beast was a wolf.

   I was frightened, angry and sad, and felt as if
   the old familiar world had blown away
   and I was standing in another world
   where I could imagine the old engines of fate
   whirring and clanking somewhere, out of sight.
   Slowly the world came back, and we were in it,
   however lost. We didn't say very much.
   I think we both felt sorry for each other,
   and I think that both of us knew our marriage was over.

6. I am trying to sleep after a long day
   in the hospital. For an hour early this morning,
   I tried to resuscitate a six-month old,
   a baby boy who was found dead in his crib
   when his mother woke up and went to give him his bottle.
   This afternoon, in the space of one hour,
   three patients arrived in cardiac arrest.
   Eventually, I pronounced all of them dead.
   I feel as if I'm stained with blood and death
   and feel as if I want to sleep forever.
   When I'm almost asleep, I hear my daughter Rachel
   start to cry. I walk into her room
   and we get settled in the rocking chair.
   She puts her head on my shoulder. I start to sing.
   Then I hear the owl outside her window,
   the owl that lives in the old cedar tree.
   I stop singing, and tell her about the owl,
   and she picks her head up, and listens for a while,
   then smiles at me, and puts her head back down,
   and I go on singing until she falls asleep.

Looking At An Old Photograph With My Four Year Old Daughter, Sara

Sara, where do you think you were before you were born?
I was at Baskin-Robbins.

Sara brings me a framed photograph
taken at Christmas, several years ago,
that shows me standing in front of the Christmas tree
with Sean and Michael, Uncle Dick and Jack.
She looks at the picture and asks me, "Where am I?"
I tell her the picture was taken before she was born.
"I was just a twinkle in your eye?"
I laugh, wondering who might have told her this.
"You were just a twinkle in my eye."
But she goes on staring at the photograph
as if she could find herself in her father's eyes.
How certain she is that she was always here,
that she belongs here, that she will always be here.

The Game Of Go

Many years ago,
for Christmas, someone gave me
the ancient game of Go.
This will be fun, I thought.
I liked the stark beauty
of the black and white stones.

In the instruction booklet,
I found this warning:
The rules for the game of Go
are simple and easy to learn.
However, the game itself
is sufficiently complex
that no one can hope to master it
within his lifetime.

Where did they get this horseshit?,
I thought to myself. And then
I played several games
and decided they were right.

The game has been put away
for years in my study closet,
but still it calls to me,
like the orphans in Viet Nam,
like a career in neurosurgery,
like adultery.

Trying To Stop Smoking

I am trying to stop smoking Camels again
and my sense of personal integrity is gone.
No longer one person, suddenly I'm a crowd,
The man with the iron will appears and dissolves.
The addict picks up the cigarette and lights it.
The connoisseur of fine Turkish tobacco
inhales a lungful of smoke and begins to smile.
The guilty bystander watches all this happen,
wringing his hands, thinking about cancer,
chronic lung disease and heart attacks.
The almost neutral observer writes this down.

Samuel Johnson, Describing Meaningless Activity

Sir, this is like getting on horseback on a ship.
So is being born. And all the rest of your life.

Monsters

You might have seen these things
in museums: the child with two heads,
the anencephalic child,
the cyclops. Safe and remote,
they float in glass jars
of pale, discolored liquids.

The child is about to be born
in the delivery room.
The mother has read books
like *Childbirth Without Fear*.
Now she is working hard,
gripping the hand of the father
who is standing beside her.
A camera hangs from his neck.

The child is in my hands.
No one dares to speak.

The woman screams,
Show me my baby!!

We gather around the monster
like a coven of witches,
our mouths shut tight, our eyes
shining with love and fury.

Road Burns

The paramedics bring our patient in.
When we peel off the bloody clothes, we find his tattoos.
Big blue letters across his back spell out
the words, HELL'S ANGEL. Across his left forearm,
it says, LET'S FUCK; across the right, EAT PUSSY.

He is in his late thirties, losing his hair,
overweight. I think he looks like me.
Please give me something for this goddamn pain!
We give him a generous dose of Demerol
and swab Lidocaine over the raw skin.

A nurse gently scrubs his numb wounds with a toothbrush.
"Haven't heard too much from you boys lately."
"No, I guess we've been getting kind of sneaky."
When the nurse is done, he's bandaged with Silvadene
and then sent home with some pills to take for the pain.

We laugh about his tattoos after he's gone.
Looking into his future, I see a man
wearing long sleeves to his daughter's First Communion,
or arriving at a hospital like this one,
after a stroke, perhaps, when he's eighty-one.

When they take the clothes off his decrepit body,
someone will laugh, but also feel uneasy,
the way I felt today, looking at him,
thinking about the lives there must have been,
quietly falling apart, under his skin.

There Are A Million Stories

I walk into room A
to see the woman with the injured ribs.
I ask her what happened, and she smiles,
and then she tells me her story.
I work at the newspaper.
This man works next to me.
I've known him for one year
and he seemed very nice, he was always nice to me.
Today when he came to work, he was quiet,
he looked very unhappy.
So I said, "What's wrong with you?"
He didn't answer. He just glared at me.
Suddenly he slapped the Chinaman in the face
and when the Chinaman tried to hit him back,
he grabbed me tight around my ribs
and squeezed so hard I thought he was trying to kill me.
He was standing so close
I could feel his privates against my leg.
They got him off me, finally.
Then he pulled his pants down.
Of course, the Chinaman turned away
because he didn't want to see that.
The police came and took him somewhere.
My ribs were sore, but now I feel OK.
I feel sorry for the man. He just went crazy.
What would make a person act like that?

I shake my head and shrug, as puzzled as she is,
and examine her ribs, and tell her she'll be all right.
She smiles again, she looks very happy,
and I think today is a day she will always remember.
Something strange and frightening happened
but she survived it, she is all right,
and she will tell this story over and over.

I walk into room B
and see a Chinese man with a bruised face...

After Seeing A Man On Television Who Had Been Struck By Lightning Eleven Times

Imagine how it feels
when the sky begins to darken,
and the black cloud-mountains
hammer their kettle-drums,
and that old power and light
starts streaking across the heavens
on its way down,
looking for him again.

Christmas Eve, Wrapping The Children's Presents

I want to give you something like peace, or like joy,
things that no one can give to anyone,
but I wrap up all of your toys that will break, or get lost,
and wonder who it is that is hurt the most.

Memories From Childhood: The Night Of The Rosenberg Execution

A hot evening in June. I was nine years old.
My father and I were sitting on the grass
in the backyard, watching the dark shadows
spreading across the lawn as the sun went down.
A Yankee game was on the radio.
Mantle, or Maris, had slammed a long home run,
and I was trying to sound like Mel Allen,
the way he said, *Going, going, gone.*
Suddenly the game was interrupted
by a news bulletin. The announcer said,
Julius and Ethel Rosenberg are dead.
Then he went on to describe the execution.
Julius was lead into the death chamber
and strapped into the electric chair.
A heavy black hood was dropped over his head
before the executioner pulled the switch.
Julius was electrocuted first,
and then Ethel, in the same electric chair,
a short time later. Ethel was shocked twice.
When she was examined after the first shock,
the doctor said he could hear her heart still beating.

Later that evening, when I went to bed,
Ozzie and Harriet were on the radio.
I heard their voices, the sound of canned laughter.
My father and mother were in the living room
and their voices sounded faint and far away.
Through the window above my bed, I could see the sky.
The moon seemed brighter than a hundred watt bulb
and clouds were scattered around like soiled rags.
A moth was beating its wings against the screen.
It was a hot night, and I couldn't sleep,
and I lay in the dark for hours, soaked with sweat,
feeling my heart pounding in my chest,
wondering how it had started, how it would stop.

Memories From Childhood: Grandmother

You kept so many together
in your grand old house.
You taught me the clouds and the flowers
and most of my first words.
Now that you are dead
and buried under flowers
I no longer remember the names of,
I can find no words
to bring you back to me.
I am still the child
who followed you down to the cellar
where you shoveled coal in winter
into the big, black furnace.
Standing safely behind you,
blinking against the heat,
I was amazed you were able to keep
such a great fire going.

Recurring Dreams

1. The first day of school, I am walking home in the rain,
   wearing a yellow raincoat. It is dark.
   Lights are coming on in all the houses
   but I seem to know that all of them are empty.
   When I get to my house, I can see it is dark inside.
   It looks as if it's been abandoned for years.
   The magnolia tree in the front yard is in bloom
   and the petals seem to glow with their own light.
   The rain falls faster and harder. After a while,
   there is only water and darkness and a deep silence
   except for a muffled sound like someone's heart.

2. I am in a rowboat with friends, at night, on a river.
   We have stopped rowing, and it is hard to tell
   if the boat is moving at all. All we can see
   is the moon, and the moonlight shining on the water.
   All of a sudden, the river disappears
   a few yards in front of the boat. I recognize
   the sound of water roaring over the falls,
   and then the sickening roller-coaster drop
   that is like a perfect memory, but of what?

Old Story

The prince goes through fire and water and kills the dragon
and comes to the princess sleeping in her castle.
He kisses the princess, she turns into a frog,
and he goes out looking for another one,
until all the princesses are gone.

Night School

Here we are again, trying to understand our story
in the calm light of eternity, but shamelessly distracted
by the anthropomorphic clouds, the falling leaves,
the slow and sexual veronica of August

as it turns into September and October,
the cape swirling around, the future snorting through.
A cloud of dust rises and settles down. Everyone's gone home.
Then there are tears, regrets, hideous handkerchiefs.

A man from Kansas drives out of the Hudson Tunnel
and looks at New York lit up like a monument.
How in the name of Christ did this get here?, he wonders,
lost in the stream of history and bad traffic.

But back to our story, what do you think will happen?
We are always ready to be amazed, we know our struggles
will have an uncertain outcome, but will finally be over,
and no one will survive to remember.

Kafka

How to go on, into oblivion,
not knowing why you were born, or who you are?

I think of Kafka, waking to blood on his pillow,
the daily horror of the sputum jar.

Buried Alive

One cloudy Tuesday, they drove past a cemetery,
and he said to his wife, "Would you like to be buried here?"
It looked like a peaceful place, with its green lawns,
and the gray headstones arranged in careful rows
under the ancient branches of oaks and elms.
"No, I don't want to be buried here," she said.
"I don't want to be buried anywhere. I'm afraid
of being buried alive." He laughed. "It happens,"
she said. "I've read about it. And if I'm dead,
I still don't want to be put under the ground.
I know it's crazy, but it frightens me.
Doesn't it bother you?" He laughed again,
his eyes on the dark road in front of him.
"No," he said, "I'm looking forward to it."

Some Nights

Nothing has happened, nothing is happening,
nothing is going to happen. What do you want?

Some nights your heart feels like a dark ocean,
a calm ocean, dreaming of tidal waves.

Tonight

Tonight I woke up from a dream of pure longing,
a desire I can feel with my whole body,
even now, now that I'm wide awake,
but not a desire for anything I can name.
It feels like gravity, the way I imagine
gravity would feel, as an emotion.
I look out my bedroom window and see the moon,
the full moon shining in a grotto of clouds.
In the fields across from my house, coyotes howl.
Perhaps they are howling their hearts out at the moon
but who knows what inspires them to howl?
I am quiet as usual, wanting to understand
why I had this dream, why it woke me up,
and I think that tomorrow, in the hospital,
I will appear to know exactly what I'm doing,
and even feel as if I know, but tonight
I feel lost in this world, and I think the moon
is like the light at the end of a long tunnel.

One Man Walking

One man walking down a country road
with fields on either side, gold and brown.
Off in the distance, hills, and patches of trees.

A day in late summer or early fall,
a very hot day, the sunlight beating down
from the blue sky, where the clouds haven't moved for hours.

There is nothing here to tell what year it is,
or where the road comes from, or where it goes,
or why the man is out walking alone

in a scene so calm and still, like a photograph,
it almost seems that time has been escaped from,
and nothing will ever change or ever happen.

A truck roars past, raising a cloud of dust.
The man waves at the truck, but no one waves back.
And the dust hangs in the air a long time.

In The Small Town Of Claremont, As Summer Begins To Turn Into Autumn, The Apprentice Finally Gets To Meet The Master. Moved, He Composes These Simple Quatrains In Admiration, Respect And Gratitude

for Bob Mezey

If you can find some pleasure in my lines,
and laugh out loud, or maybe shed some tears,
you should, with Justice, feel a little proud.
You have been teaching me for many years.

I have often come to your poems for my mind's pleasure,
for lessons in the art of rhyme and measure.
And I have tried to write as well as you.
Few poets can. I still have work to do.

To A Dear Friend Who Is Living Far Away

after an ancient Chinese poem by Po Chui
for Bob Mezey

Only a year ago, I met a friend,
a master in the art of poetry.
I had been reading his books since I was young,
and many of the poems I knew by heart.
My poems were clearly the work of an apprentice
but he was kind and generous to me
and welcomed me as a fellow in the art.
Many the hours we charmed with talk of verse.
We quoted favorite lines to one another,
often the other's favorites as well.
Some well-loved poems we would recite together
as if we were chanting scripture, or a prayer.
Long ago, a poet friend once asked him,
How many people in the world tonight
are thinking about the meters? We thought about them,
we talked about them. Hell, we reveled in them,
with *the love that masquerades as pure technique.*
I think back often to the night we met
and started talking about poetry.
The doors of Heaven opened in my mind.
I would have laughed, had someone told me then
that after only one brief year had gone,
I would be struggling with how to say farewell
to someone I had simply grown to love
as a father, brother, teacher and dear friend.
Tonight I dreamed that he was back in Claremont
and I saw again the face of a dear friend.
He seemed to be saying that nothing had really changed.
Words can travel at the speed of light
and we will go on talking as before.
I woke up, and thought he was still talking to me.
I turned on the light. There was no one there at all.
On a night like tonight, missing his company,
I will sit at my wooden table under the trees.
A candle will illuminate the page
on which I'll write some words to send to him,
hoping to make him smile, and touch his heart.

Doctor

The nurse's face looks frightened when she tells me
I need to see the patient in Room 1.
I go with her and introduce myself
to the silent man lying on his back,
and lift the bloody towel that hides his face.
Cancer has been eating at his face
and the left side of it is nearly gone,
now little more than an ugly, bloody crater.
He has lost his left eye, part of his nose,
and the left side of his mouth. He opens his eye,
and lifts his right hand up in front of it.
He is holding a small mirror in his hand
and stares into the mirror at his face.
He drops his hand, then lifts it up again,
he does this over and over. I take the mirror
and look into the glass, and see my face.
He reaches for the mirror, and I ask him,
"Why do you want to torture yourself this way?"

He smiles at me. I think it is a smile.
"I am not trying to torture myself, Doctor.
I am teaching myself to want to die."
I think of the Latin root of the word, "Doctor,"
an ancient Latin verb that means "to teach."
I think of nothing I can teach this man.
He is teaching me, a painful lesson
that he has suffered long to learn by heart.
I want to help. I want to do no harm.
I give him back his mirror, touching his hand,
and watch him lift his hand up to his eye
and go staring at his ruined face,
the mirror telling the plain and awful truth.

After Reading A Book Of Old Chinese Poetry, I Stay Awake Tonight And Write This Poem

A beautiful place is the town of Lo-Yang.
The big streets are full of spring light.
—Wen-Ti, 5th century, CE

A beautiful place is the little town of Claremont.
The quiet streets are lined by ancient trees.
Down the long avenues of old houses,
pepper trees, sycamores, cedars, oaks and elms,
eucalyptus, palms and jacarandas,
translate sunlight into restful shadows.
Flowers are everywhere, and citrus trees.
Lemons and oranges ornament the gardens.
Students walk by, with their books, to the colleges.
Townspeople walk together to the village.
From parks and schoolyards, children's voices call.
Sunday mornings, churches ring their their bells.
On a clear day, you can see the mountains
where children play, in winter, in the snow,
and long trails lead to streams and waterfalls.
Deer and mountain lions walk the mountains.
Rattlesnakes doze for hours in the sun.
Some days the ponds are visited by bears
who stumble home with their bellies full of trout.
Unable to sleep, I leave my house tonight
and sit at my wooden table under the trees.
Now the winds and birds have settled, the night is still.
The owl in the cedar tree begins to bell.
Rose and jasmine burn their their sticks of incense.
Moonlight falls on Claremont through the clouds.
I remember Po Chui's poem about the cranes.
In the early dusk, down an alley of green moss,
the garden boy is leading the cranes home.
How strange and powerful, the love of home.
Stranger still, to be alive at all,
to be anywhere, in all its endless detail,
and the millions of tiny locks that will be broken
before you can be released from where you are,
to return again forever to the place,
so many years ago, you started from,
the nothing that is everywhere but here.

Hotel

After a poem by Donald Justice, with the same title,
the same form, and the same last line

One night, it seemed this grand and secret place
was their whole world, in which they felt at home,
walking down long halls to find their room.
Later, waiting for sleep, waiting for dawn,
it seemed the sounds of the city had been turned on,
horns and sirens blaring far away,
and planes droning past in the night sky
that they had almost forgotten was still there.
And then, at dawn, how strange to wake up here.

And not so grand and secret, after all,
they may have felt, walking through the lobby
and stopping in the little shop for coffee.
Beyond the plate-glass window was the world,
remembered now. Soon they would be hurled
into the daily storms and battles there.
And home seemed far away now, very far.
Perhaps she shed some tears, but silently.
And all was as it had been and would be.

A Brief Inferno

*In the middle of my life, I had lost my way,
and found myself alone in a dark wood.*
                                    −Dante

Of course, we are always alone, always lost,
and always in the middle of our lives.
At least we hope there is enough time left
to finally get things right. If only, if only...

And the dark wood seems to be getting darker
as we try to find the path we wandered from.
The world looks strange and wild when you are lost.
Waiting somewhere out there is the witch.

You get up in the morning and you drive to work,
your eyes on the road, your hands gripping the wheel.

The Moon Of Creagan

There is nothing in books, only a few words.
—Robert Mezey

Walking out of my house early this morning,
I glanced up at the sky and saw the moon.
The world was full of light from a brilliant sun,
but the moon was a pale circle of gray and white,
as if it had been burning up all night
until, by morning, it was a small ash
left in the deep blue bowl of the cloudless sky.

Though I must have seen this moon before,
today I felt the thrill of recognition.
This is the moon of ash, the moon of Creagan.
I thought of Borges' poems about the moon,
his wish to say its true and secret name.
There are so many names, but with just one,
you can hang the moon in the sky over the poem,
shining in the radiance of its name.

Anyone who spends much time with words
will often wonder how they work their magic,
and understand the allure of the Kabballah.
These little strings of consonants and vowels
are all we need to dream the dreams of Shakespeare
and write the history of recorded time
and everything that we have learned so far
about the inexhaustible universe,
and everything we have so far left unsaid.
With the simple magic of the alphabet,
a poem can cast a spell down years of time,
as long as words are loved, as long as rhyme.

Years from now, in a quiet library,
paging through an old anthology,
someone may find these lines and see the moon
shining still in the sky over the poem.

I like to think the thrill will feel the same
as the thrill I felt today, in a distant time,
as, entering the story of the poem,
he will walk out of my house into the sun,
and glance up at the sky and see the moon,
and recognize the moon, and know its name.

Another Riddle

It would shatter us to know wholly our nature;
Out of his pity for us, God has given
Day after day, and then oblivion.

–Borges, from *Oedipus And The Riddle,*
translated by Mezey and Barnes

They knew in the beginning what had started
and this strange knowledge frightened the best of them.
They locked it up and tried not to remember.
For years the memory still could make them tremble.
But this died out. And as the years came on,
by steady work, new rooms of thought to move in,
new pictures to be hung on all the walls,
were added to the house of intellect.

After how many years, we go on working,
knowing as we live from day to day
that night is coming, and oblivion.
And sometimes, when the fragile lights are out,
we hear that scratching in the attic room.
It lives in the same house. How many midnights
have we paused on the stairs up to its door
and turned back, shaking, to our quiet beds?

Haiku

Words on the page like
stones on the streambed, your mind
flowing over them.

The quiet garden.
Falling asleep in sunlight,
before the hailstorm.

Sky of loud fire,
skyrockets, Roman candles.
And my dog, trembling.

Night. Loud orchestra
of frogs in the little pond,
suddenly quiet.

My African Grey,
Earl, looks formal, elegant,
singing Duke Of Earl.

The movie playing
tonight in the old folks home
is *Forever Young*.

Bombay sapphire, so
beautiful a name for this
clear fire-water.

Great Wall of China,
only man-made object you
can see from the moon.

Waking in our bed,
I reach for her, remember
she has gone away.

Saw my face today
in the mirror, recognized
someone I once knew.

Tumor in your lung.
What help now, the flea circus
of philosophy?

Reading over my
poems, always the same thought. So
much has been left out.

Even the atoms
are tired tonight, the quarks
turning off their charm.

What I am will soon
be gone, and then forgotten,
and my grave empty.

Jacarandas

The jacarandas are in bloom again
and lavender blossoms are falling everywhere,
announcing the beginning of summer here,
in Claremont, California, this small town
of old houses, colleges and trees,
where I have lived for over thirty years.
In early June, the blossoms bloom and fall,
each lavender blossom like a little bell,
and their summer anniversary makes me smile.
Some hidden rhythm at the heart of things
summons them here each year to light and glory,
but the flowers bloom for only a little while,
and I am also in this rhythm's thrall,
and know, one summer, when the flowers come,
no one will find me here at this address.
A fading memory then, my name and face.

Some hidden rhythm at the heart of things
brings lavender blossoms snowing everywhere.
Days are passing, brief and beautiful.
The jacarandas are in bloom again.

A Good Day

The hot sun had gone down
at the end of a summer's day.
Good friends had gone home
and the children had gone to bed.
All the afternoon winds
had blown away somewhere,
and the world was clear and calm.
We were happy then
to let the evening come, to sit outside at dusk
and watch the brush of darkness
touch the lawn and the trees,
and then the wall and the sky,
until it was finally night.
Some nights you would light a candle,
some nights we had the moon
and the sky was full of stars.
We would sit together and talk
until the words ran out,
and then we would come inside
and listen for the children,
safe and asleep in their beds.
We would make love then
and snuggle into sleep,
but before we fell asleep,
one of us would say,
Today was a good day,
and then the other would answer,
Yes. Yes it was.

Road Kill

You may have thought things would come right again
If only you could sit quite still and wait.
                                            —Larkin

Driving to the hospital late last night,
I turned down a road that ran between dark fields.
Up ahead, in the middle of the road,
a small brown rabbit was sitting very still,
looking down at a rabbit who was dead,
a mangled corpse, run over by a car.
Lit up by my headlights, he took off toward the fields.
Slowing down, I drove by the dead rabbit,
then stopped the car, and watched in the rear-view mirror.
The rabbit came back and sat in the road again,
resuming the vigil for his dead friend, or kin.
Quiet, still, he sat and stared at him.

Touched, unable to guess what you felt or thought,
I found it hard to watch you suffer this.
You have no words to understand what death is,
no words to ease your sadness, to console,
to mourn or pray, or tell your friend farewell.

I hope you made it safely home last night
and woke this morning in the warm sunlight.
This morning, at my table under the trees,
because you have no words, I've written these.

Jorge Luis Borges
1899-1986

for Bob Mezey, with many thanks for his
wonderful translations of Borges

You have escaped the labyrinth of time,
escaped your poems, your stories and your name.
Your name, with its two dates, is carved in stone,
and printed here, on this page as white as stone,
but you have journeyed to oblivion.
No one will come here looking for your tomb,
and no one will find you there. Where you have gone,
no one can find your now but in a dream.

Dreams and mirrors always haunted you.
This poem will be a dream and mirror too.
In its flawed glass, let those who come here view
the images that consoled and tortured you.
Here is the moon, the tiger and the rose,
here the river of Heraclitus flows,
and each metonymic sword and dagger glows
with tales of the brave captains, toughs or gauchos.

Here is the labyrinth and library,
the books you loved and, finally, could not see,
the histories of algebra and fire,
and music that reflects time in its mirror,
the atlases, theologies, and Shakespeare,
the chronicles of dynasties and war,
and Plato's ancient dreams about the pure,
Eternal Forms your father found so dear.

Here, your last evening counting syllables
and shuffling rhymes until they chime like bells,
and the last time you sacrifice a pawn,
knowing the logic of the endgame soon
will force the now inevitable checkmate,
the mirror and the metaphor of fate.
The bar of sulfur glowing in a closet,
the treasured colors of your last sunset,

your father's face, kissed for the last time,
the mirrored face of Borges, growing dim,
but grave and calm, as you said farewell to him,
the last evening you waited for the dawn
so you could feel the blessing of the sun,
these memories now live only in a poem.
How many memories vanished with your ghost,
like flowers pressed in a well-loved book, and lost?

Alone, in a strange city, far from home,
awake all night, and waiting for the dawn,
but hoping for the calm of sleep to come,
why do I go on working on this poem?
Why do I suddenly feel I am no one,
that it is Borges, wherever he has gone,
into the secret night of oblivion,
who whispers these dear words that I write down?

Lines Written In A Bad Mood, To The Muse

I wanted to leave you. I missed my chance.
Now you have me by the balls.

For you, each night, I go out and dance,
on the tightrope, over the falls.

After Reading A Review Of A Book Of Poems Which Is Praised For Being Free Of The Old Confines Of Rhyme, Free Of The More Rigid Forms Poetry Commanded In The Past

This book won a major prize, was highly praised.
Skeptical, but hoping to be surprised,
I bought the book, came home and read it through.
I should have known better. Here is *my* review.

Free from all the fetters of form and rhyme,
imagination, humor, wit and skill,
these are not poems at all, except in name.
Who'll read these poems with pleasure? No one will.

Some poets still are masters of the art.
If you want the real thing, this is where to start.
Read Justice, Mezey, Snodgrass, Wilbur, Hecht,
Borges, Larkin, Hall and Gunn, Coulette,
Frost and Stevens, Robinson and Hardy,
Miller Williams, Starbuck, Kennedy,
Barnes and Fairchild, J. V. Cunningham,
The Art Of The Lathe, The Exclusions Of A Rhyme.
Reading these books, I know what to expect,
familiar poems, with the power to touch me yet.

All the old masters I won't mention here,
just Martial and Catullus, Horace, Homer,
Po Chui and Chaucer, Donne and Wyatt, Shakespeare.

These are the poems I keep returning to
when I close an artless book, one more disaster.
And then I find what I am looking for,
artful free verse, poems in rhyme and measure,
instruction and delight, and the deep pleasure
of real poetry written by a master,
strong and clear and memorable and true.
The art is old. The poems are fresh and new.

Driving Down A Country Road In The Rain

Today we drove in the rain down a country road,
with fields on either side turning to mud
where cows were standing still in the cold rain.
My daughter saw the cows and said, *How cute!*.

I told her I thought the cows might be depressed.
If the pastures were sprayed with Prozac, would the cows
run and frolic over the wet grass,
lifting their heads, licking at the rain?

We laughed, but I was reminded of the days
when I felt like a dusty field turning to mud,
or like a dumb beast standing in the rain.

Caveman

Last night I had a dream about a caveman,
coming back from a long, unlucky hunt,
tired and thirsty, finding his long way home.
When he gets home, he learns his wife has been raped,
and both her legs are broken. Some of his children
have been killed, and all the rest are dying,
and someone has shit in his cistern of rainwater.
With a rock, he helps his wife and children die,
then digs a hole with the rock and his bare hands,
so he can bury them. When he is finished,
he stands by himself and looks up at the stars
that have no names, not even the name *star*,
not knowing why, or what he's looking for.

Another Love Story

My girlfriend dumped me for a guy named Frank
and my heart did all the things a heart can do,
when it is broken. Long nights, alone, I drank,
in my house that started smelling like a zoo,
wondering how my girl, whose love seemed true,
could leave me suddenly for someone new.

A few months later, I saw my former lover,
and could tell my hardest times were nearly over
as a great idea blossomed in my head.
Laughing, I walked up to her and said,
working my eyebrows in my best Groucho,
Hello, sweetheart, can I be Frank with you?

Poem For My Dentist

This poem's for Dr. Gregrey F. Bodhaine.
Some poets might suspect that I'm insane
for using the austere art of formal verse
for one who drills, or pulls, my teeth, or worse.
I don't much care. You have been good to me.
You are a wizard of good dentistry.

Your skill and sense of humor help me smile.
I'm thankful for the magic you can do,
and hope this light verse brings a smile to you.
It's fun to play with words a little while,
forget the dreadful music of the drill,
the horror of decay, the root canal.

Before I met you, I would quake with fear,
whenever I approached a dentist's chair.
But at your hands, I've suffered little pain.
You're a master in the art of Novocaine.

Over the years, my teeth have gone to hell,
in spite of cleanings, flossing, fluoride gel.
You've done your best to help my teeth get well,
a losing battle, started much too late.
Each morning, I put in my upper plate,
and think of all the work still left to do.
I'm off tomorrow. I'll be calling you.

Telephone Greeting

You have reached 985-0732,
and so you have my number. This is true,
but I'm not here right now to talk to you.
I'm sure you know exactly what to do.

Please leave your number and your name, OK?
Then say whatever the hell you want to say.
The secret games that the electrons play
will save your words. Sometime later today,

when I get home, or struggle out of bed,
when I sober up, and finally clear my head,
my laundry's done, and all my books are read,
when all the cows come home, and God is dead,

my taxes paid, my accounts all in the black,
I'll check my messages, and call you back.

Fooling Around With The Words
In The Good Book

Many are called, but few are chosen.
Many are cold, but few are frozen.

And death shall come like a thief in the night.
Please come tonight, and take my wife.

Abandon all you have and follow me.
Homeless, lost, in utter penury,
will it help to contemplate the Trinity,
the Father and the Son, the Holy Ghost?
It little matters, since we'll soon be toast.

Blessed are the meek, for they shall inherit the earth.
So will the proud, the arrogant, the dull,
the heretic, the insanely criminal.
Let's not mince words. The earth inherits us.
All saints and sinners ride the same damned bus.

All of us one day will be underground.
On Judgement Day, if the angels' trumpets sound,
it will not matter; we will never hear,
nor rise in rapture. We will stay right here.

Father, father, why have you forsaken me?
Nothing personal, Son. I do it randomly.

I am the Lord thy God. I can do whatever I want.
It's not in the Book, but it's my favorite taunt.
Lighten up, and laugh, as all my angels do.
I've made you in my image, as you know.
Your Creator has a sense of humor too.
Rabbis and priests have been too hard on you.
Forget the Ten Commandments, and the Torah,
and book a two week cruise to Bora Bora.
Just remember to be kind to one another,
and kiss your kids today. And call your mother.

My Patient In Room One Today

There was an old pervert from Serbia
who whipped out his dick, in suburbia.
Some kid called the cops,
and they collared old Pops.
Now his dick will no longer disturb ya.

Snapshots From New Orleans

Last night, I photographed my teenage daughters
in a small, dark restaurant on Bourbon Street.
Sara and Rachel smiled at me. They were framed
by the wide window behind them, thrown open now
to the revelry and chaos on the street.
Their faces looked like masks of white enamel
in the eerie illumination of the flash.
I went on snapping their pictures in the dark.
Not innocent myself, nor sentimental,
I was surprised when it began to feel
like photographing angels lost in Hell.

Rain is falling now on New Orleans,
falling on its balconies and flowers,
wrought-iron gates that open into gardens,
on drunks vomiting in the old, bricked alleys,
the addicts pushing needles in their veins,
on a teenage girl who cruises Bourbon street
and lifts her blouse until she scores some beads.

Girls prowl the streets all night like feral cats.
Now one is cornered by a pack of men,
chanting, over and over, *Show us your tits!!*
She obliges them, and shows them more than that.
So many girls look younger than my daughters.
I imagine some are homeless, runaways.
Do fathers somewhere pray they're safe tonight?
My daughters still are innocent, I think,
as were these others once, not long ago.
A father is no protection for his children.
Here with my daughters, I am praying too.

For My Daughter, Sara,
On Her Nineteenth Birthday

I had flown back from Chicago late one night
and drove home from the airport into Claremont.
In the old, dark house on Kemper Avenue,
I found your mother in the library,
sitting under a lamp, reading a book.
We hugged and kissed. I sat down next to her
and started telling her about Chicago.
She listened quietly, and smiled at me.
I am pregnant with our daughter, Sara.
I was suddenly filled with so much happiness
but couldn't find the words to tell her this.
I walked across the room to the fireplace,
and watched the fire burn, and felt its heat,
and then came back and looked into her eyes.
And the great wheels smash and pound beneath our feet,
is what I finally said, smiling at her,
a line from Thomas Wolfe, and Donald Justice.
I have never been so happy, ever again,
unless perhaps on your and Rachel's birthdays.
My hands were the first hands to ever touch you.
I delivered you, then clamped and cut the cord,
then gave you to your mother. She held you, smiling,
and I was smiling, and Dick and Marilyn.
Perhaps you still remembered the dark ocean,
so calm, so lately crossed. Now you were loved,
in a world in which you felt that you belonged.

You and I were watching television
a few years later. You were sitting on my lap.
We were watching a situation comedy
that showed a dead man in a funeral home.
You started to cry, said, *I don't want to die.*
I laughed. *Sara, you're only four years old,*
with a long and happy life in front of you.
I know, you said, *but someday I will be old,*
and I will be alone, I will be dying,
and then there will be no one who can help me.
Your tears fell. You were inconsolable.
I held you tight, but found no words to say.
These are the words I want to say tonight.

Though I don't want to die, someday I will.
I want you and Rachel to be with me then.
We will help each other say our last farewell,
and I will hold your hands, and die in peace,
knowing I was blessed to be your father.

When you are dying, I will be with you.
You will remember me, and know I loved you,
and remember others who are dear to you.
You will feel tired, and then more tired still.
No longer frightening, or terrible,
death will seem a friend who'll come to fetch you
from a world where you no longer feel at home.
The day will come when you will feel it's best
to close your eyes at last, and finally rest.

A few years later, one sunny afternoon,
I sat on the grass under the Kafir plum tree,
watching you and Rachel as you danced
on the patio outside the Kemper sun-room.
Marvin Gaye was on the radio,
singing, *Sexual Healing*. You sang along
with Marvin Gaye, dancing with your sister,
and I watched and smiled, and wondered, and still do.

Then, a few years later, you came to tell me
that you were going to run away from home.
Where will you sleep?, I said. *What will you eat?*
We went into the kitchen, and ate our dinner,
and then you said it was time for you to go.
You packed some clean clothes in your little backpack,
and said good-bye, looking brave and sad.
I picked you up, and held you in my arms.
I told you I wanted you to stay with us.
You started crying; I carried you up to bed,
and watched you then until you fell asleep.

A few years later, you were at Carden School.
I was the one who had run away from home,
living by myself, apart from you.
You sang a solo in a musical,
and I was there to hear you sing your song.
How beautifully you sang, and stopped the show,
as everyone told me, after you were done.

Later that evening, when I went to bed,
I heard you singing as I fell asleep.

The years pass, but they are years, and full.
I can remember when you learned to talk,
how thrilled I was to hear you say my name.
Last year I watched you graduate from high school
and now you're off to college, doing well.
Some weekends you drive home to visit us,
and Ricky, your sister Rachel, your boyfriend, Andrew.

Life is a short night in a bad hotel,
St. Theresa may have said. Life is, as well,
the million-petalled flower of being here.
Thank you for coming here to be with us.
Life is a short night in a bad hotel.
Make a mantra of this bagatelle,
and chant it daily. It will help you smile,
and use the time that has been given you,
a gift more precious since it cannot last,
to work and love, to suffer joy and pain,
on the path you will walk down once, and never again.

You're beautiful, Sara, with eyes of the clearest blue,
eyes that can see into the tears of things,
and still light up with love and laughter too.
Dear, good daughter, I am proud of you.

My Parrots Talking To Each Other

Earl and Lola live in separate cages
in the same room. Earl is an African Grey,
formal, elegant, and very smart.
His feathers are gray, his tail-feathers are red.
Lola is an Amazon, colorful,
blue and green and yellow. She is bubbly,
very flirtatious, and she likes to sing.
Earl is laconic, with a good sense of humor,
and often speaks in my voice, which is low and dry.
One night I was reading in the living room
and heard my parrots talking to each other.
Hello, Earl, Lola's here, say Hi
to Lola. Come on, Earl, say Hi to Lola.
Then Lola starts to sing, like a coloratura.
Earl interrupts her singing, and says, *What?*,
in my voice. Lola laughs, and tries again.
Hi Earl, Lola's here. Say Hi to Lola.
And then she sings. Earl listens for a while
and then he says, *Be quiet*. Lola laughs
and goes on singing. Earl listens again,
and then he raises his voice and yells, *Stop it!!*
Lola ends her song. Now she is quiet.
Earl laughs, and then he says to Lola, *Bummer*.